THE FREEING OF THE DUST

Books by Denise Levertov

Poetry

The Double Image

Here and Now

Overland to the Islands

With Eyes at the Back of Our Heads

The Jacob's Ladder

O Taste and See

The Sorrow Dance

Relearning the Alphabet

To Stay Alive

Footprints

The Freeing of the Dust

Prose

The Poet in the World

Translations

Guillevic/Selected Poems

Denise Levertov

The Freeing of the Dust

A New Directions Book

ACKNOWLEDGMENTS
Some of the poems in this book first appeared in the following publications: *American Report, The Archive, Clifton, Cold Mountain Press, Confrontation, Copper Canyon, Field, Hearse, 100 Flowers, I Pass Behind Your Mirror, Images, Jam To-Day, Lakes and Prairies, The Lamp in the Spine, Lemming, Madrona, Mundus Artium, New Directions in Prose and Poetry 29, Paintbrush, Phoebe, The Shore Review, Southern Review* (Australia), *Squeezebox, Stuffed Crocodile, West End.*

"The Distance" first appeared in *Poetry*.

Manufactured in the United States of America
First published clothbound and as ND Paperbook 401 in 1975
Published simultaneously in Canada by McClelland & Stewart, Ltd.

Library of Congress Cataloging in Publication Data

Levertov, Denise, 1923-
    The freeing of the dust.

    (A New Directions Book)
    Poems.
    I. Title.
PR6023.E88F7   811'.5'4   75-8568
ISBN 0–8112–0581–9
ISBN 0–8112–0582–7 pbk.

New Directions Books are published for James Laughlin
by New Directions Publishing Corporation,
333 Sixth Avenue, New York 10014

Contents

Green water of lagoons,
brown water of a great river
sunning its muscles along intelligent
rectangular swathes of
other brown, other green,
alluvial silvers.
          Always air
looked down through, gives
a reclamation of order, re-
visioning solace: the great body
not torn apart, though raked and raked
by our claws—

The turnpike, without history, a function
of history, grossly
cut through the woods,

secondgrowth woods without memory,
crowded saplings, bushes entangled,
sparse weedcrop on burned-over sandy embankments.

Brutally realized intentions speed us
from city to city—a driver's world:
and what is a driver? Driven? Obsessed?
These thickarmed men
seem at rest, assured, their world
a world of will and function.

Majestic insects buzz through the sky
bearing us pompously from love to love,
grief to grief,
                    expensively,
motes in the gaze of that unblinking eye.

Our threads of life are sewn into dark cloth,
a sleeve that hangs down over
a sinister wrist. All of us.
It must be Time whose pale fingers
dangle beneath the hem . . .

Solemn filaments, our journeyings
wind through the overcast.

Our trouble
is only the trouble anyone,
all of us, thrust from the ancient
holding-patterns, down toward
runways newbuilt,
knows; the strain
of flying wing by wing, not knowing
ever if both of us will land: the planet
under the clouds—
does it want us? Shall we be welcome,
we of air, of metallic
bitter rainbows,
of aching wings? Can we dissolve
like coins of hail,
touching down,
              down to the dense, preoccupied,
skeptical green world, that does not know us?

Night lies down
in the field when the moon
leaves. Head in clover,
held still.

It is brief,
this time of darkness,
hands of night
loosefisted, long hair
outspread.

Sooner than one would dream,
the first bird
wakes with a sobbing cry. Whitely

dew begins to drift
cloudily.
Leafily naked, forms of the world
are revealed,
all asleep. Colors

come slowly
up from behind the hilltop,
looking for forms to fill for the day,
dwellings.
Night
must rise and
move on, stiff and
not yet awake.

'Can't get that tune
out of my head,'

can't get that tree
out of

some place in me.
And don't want to:

the way it
lifts up its arms,
opens them, and—

patient the way an
elderly horse is patient—
crosses them, aloft,

to curve and recross:

the standing, the being
rooted, the look
as of longing.
At each divide,
the choice endured, branches
taking their roads in air.

Glance up
from the kitchen window;
that tree word,
still being said,
over the stone wall.

Fall mornings, its head of twigs
vaguely lifted,
a few apples
yellow in silver fog.

i

Dark, rainsoaked
oaklimbs

within thorny
auburn haze
of brush at wood's edge.

Secretly
I love you, whom
they think I have abjured.

ii

Secretly,
blueveiled
moody
autumn auburn,

you are the very wood I knew
always, that grew up
so tall, to hold at bay

the worldly princes,
baffled and torn
upon the thorns
of your redberried thickets,
may and rose.

Each day
the cardinals call and call in the rain,
each cadence scarlet
among leafless buckeye,

and passionately
the redbuds, that can't wait
like other blossoms, to flower
from fingertip twigs,
break forth

as Eve from Adam's
cage of ribs,
straight from amazed treetrunks.

Lumps of snow
are melting in tulip-cups.

The old wooden steps to the front door
where I was sitting that fall morning
when you came downstairs, just awake,
and my joy at sight of you (emerging
into golden day—
                    the dew almost frost)
pulled me to my feet to tell you
how much I loved you:

those wooden steps
are gone now, decayed,
replaced with granite,
hard, gray, and handsome.
The old steps live
only in me:
my feet and thighs
remember them, and my hands
still feel their splinters.

Everything else about and around that house
brings memories of others—of marriage,
of my son. And the steps do too: I recall
sitting there with my friend and her little son who died,
or was it the second one who lives and thrives?
And sitting there 'in my life,' often, alone or with my husband.
Yet that one instant,
your cheerful, unafraid, youthful, 'I love you too,'
the quiet broken by no bird, no cricket, gold leaves
spinning in silence down without
any breeze to blow them,
                    is what twines itself
in my head and body across those slabs of wood
that were warm, ancient, and now
wait somewhere to be burnt.

15

All one winter, in every crowded hall,
at every march and rally,
first thing I'd look for was your curly head.

One night last summer in a crowded room
across the ocean,
my heart missed a beat—it seemed I saw you
in the far corner.

You who were so many thousand miles away.

When love, exaltation, the holy awe
of Poetry entering your doors and lifting you
on one finger as if you were a feather
fallen from its wings, grasp you, then your face
is luminous. I saw the angel
of Jacob once, alabaster, stone and not stone,
incandescent.
        That look, the same,
illumines you, then.
           But when
hatred and a desire of vengeance
make you sullen, your eyes grow smaller,
your mouth turns sour, a heaviness
pulls the flesh of your poet's face
down, makes it a mask
of denial. I remember:
from the same block of stone Jacob was carved,
but he was thick, opaque. The sculptor showed
Jacob still unwounded, locked into combat, unblest,
the day
not yet dawning.

I wanted
to know all the bones of your spine, all
the pores of your skin,
tendrils of body hair.
To let
all of my skin, my hands,
ankles, shoulders, breasts,
even my shadow,
be forever imprinted
with whatever of you
is forever unknown to me.
To cradle your sleep.

You invaded my country by accident,
not knowing you had crossed the border.
Vines that grew there touched you.
                              You ran past them,
shaking raindrops off the leaves—you or the wind.
It was toward the hills you ran,
inland—

I invaded your country with all my
'passionate intensity,'
pontoons and parachutes of my blindness.
But living now in the suburbs of the capital
incognito,
                my will to take the heart of the city
                has dwindled. I love
its unsuspecting life,
its adolescents who come to tell me their dreams in the dusty park
among the rocks and benches,
I the stranger who will listen.
I love
the wild herons who return each year to the marshy outskirts.
What I invaded has
invaded me.

A story one might read and not know
                    (not have to know)
the power of the face—

    'Ten-year-old Eric
    was killed during racial tension last summer'

    Testimony . . .
    'tears . . .
    in her eyes . . .
    "I am not afraid
    of anyone.
    Nothing else
    can happen to me
    now that my son
    is dead." '

But the power is there to see, the face
of an extreme beauty, contours
of dark skin luminous
as if candles shone unflickering
on beveled oiled wood.

Her name, Alluvita,
compound of earth, river, life.

She is gazing
way beyond questioners.

Her tears
shine and don't fall.

i   America the Bountiful

After the welfare hotel
crumbled suddenly (after repeated warnings)
into the street,

Seventh Day Adventists brought supplies
of clothing to the survivors.
" 'Look at this,' exclaimed
Loretta Rollock, 48 years old,
as she held up a green dress
and lingerie. 'I've never worn
such nice clothes. I feel like
when I was a kid and my mom
brought me something.' Then
she began to cry."

ii   In the Rubble

For some the hotel's collapse meant
life would have to be started
all over again.
Sixty-year-old Charles, on welfare
like so many of the others, who said,
'We are the rootless people,' and
'I have no home, no place that I can say I
really live in,' and,
'I had become used to it here,'
also said:
'I lost
all I ever had,
in the rubble.
I lost my clothes,
I lost the picture of my parents
and I lost my television.'

24

There's a woman (you tell the gender by the noise of her heels)
lives in this 12-story building,
who won't use the elevator: hurries
down the emergency stairs from a floor higher than sixth
clop, clop, clop, every night
about the same time.
If I'm awake I hear her slowly
reascend
much later, pausing
to rest her legs
and breathe,
like someone climbing inside a monument
to see the view and say
I climbed it.
Every night.

Twisted body and whitesocked
deformed legs (evidently
too hard to get stockings on).
And little, booted, braced, feet,
swinging along
beside the crutches and under
the huge winglike shoulders . . .

Always the tap and creak and
tap and creak of
crutch and brace,
in effort always, and whirr
of wings revving up and not
getting the human, female, botched body
off the ground.
The sound never
letting up, no hushed pinewoods walk,
no slipping unseen through lakes of shadow.
Has she
some blessed deafness given
along with starved bones?
                    It seems
too much to hope.

While we lie in the road to block traffic from the air-force base,
over there the dead are strewn in the roads.

While we are carried to the bus and off to jail to be 'processed,'
over there the torn-off legs and arms of the living
hang in burnt trees and on broken walls.

While we wait and sing in ugly but not uninhabitable cells,
men and women contorted, blinded, in tiger cages, are
                                 biting their tongues
to stifle, for each other's sake, their cries of agony.
And those cruel cages are built in America.

While we refuse the standard prison liverwurst sandwiches,
knowing we'll get decent food in a matter of hours,
over there free fighters, young and old, guns never laid aside,
eat a few grains of rice and remember
Uncle Ho, and the long years he ate no better, and smile.

And while we fear
for the end of earth-life, even though we sing
and rejoice in each other's beauty and comradeship,

over there they mourn
the dead and mutilated each has seen.

They have seen and seen and heard and heard
all that we will ourselves with such effort to imagine,
to summon into the understanding . . .

And they too sing.
They too rejoice
in each other's beauty and comradeship:

they sing and fight. I see their spirits
visible, crowns of fire-thorn
flicker over their heads.

Our steps toward struggle
are like the first tottering of infant feet.
Could we,
        if life lasts
                find in ourselves
that steady courage, win
such flame-crowns?

She is weeping for her lost right arm.
She cannot write the alphabet any more
on the kindergarten blackboard.

She is weeping for her lost right arm.
She cannot hold her baby and caress it at the same time
ever again.

She is weeping for her lost right arm.
The stump aches, and her side.

She is weeping for her lost right arm.
The left alone cannot use a rifle
to help shoot down the attacking plane.

In the wide skies over the Delta
her right hand that is not there
writes indelibly,
    'Cruel America,
when you mutilate our land and bodies,
it is your own soul you destroy,
not ours.'

Because they were prisoners,
because they were polite and friendly and lonesome and homesick
because they said Yes, they knew
                                        the names of the bombs they dropped
            but didn't say whether they understood what these bombs
                                            are designed to do
                                            to human flesh, and because
        I didn't ask them, being unable to decide
        whether to ask would serve
        any purpose other than cruelty, and
because since then I met Mrs. Brown, the mother of one of
                                        their fellow prisoners,
and loved her, for she has the same lovingkindness in her
that I saw in Vietnamese women (and men too)
and because my hostility left the room and wasn't there
                                        when I thought I needed it
while I was drinking tea with the POW's,

        because of all these reasons I hope
        they were truly as ignorant,
                    as unawakened,
                                as they seemed,
I hope their chances in life up to this point
have been poor,
I hope they can truly be considered
victims of the middle America they come from,
their American Legionnaire fathers, their macho high schools,
their dull skimped Freshman English courses,

for if they did understand precisely
what they were doing, and did it anyway, and would do it again,

then I must learn to distrust
my own preference for trusting people,

then I must learn to question
my own preference for liking people,

then I must learn to keep
my hostility chained to me
so it won't leave me when I need it.

And if it is proved to me
that these men understood their acts,

how shall I ever again
be able to meet the eyes of Mrs. Brown?

Somewhere there is a dull room
where someone slow is moving,
stumbling from door to chair

to sit there patiently
doing nothing but be,
enjoying the quiet and warmth,

pleased with the gradual
slope of day's light
into his corner. Dull

illiterate saint, never imagining
the atrocious skills his kin
devise and use,

who are avidly, viciously active,
refining quality, increasing quantity—
million by million—
of standardized Agony-Inflicters.

Somewhere there is a dull room
no phosphorescence of guile illumines.
No scintillations
of cruelty.

Imagination could put forth
gentle feelers there.
Somewhere there must be

such a room, and someone dumb
in it, unknown to cruelty,
unknowing.

May Our Right Hands Lose Their Cunning

Smart bombs replace
dumb bombs. 'Now we can aim
straight into someone's kitchen.'

Hard rice
sprays out of the cooking pot
straight into the delicate jelly of eyes.

Invisible pellets,
pointed blobs of mist,
  bite through smooth pale-brown skin
  into perfect bodies,
chewing them into bloody mincemeat.
This is smart.

  There is
a dumb fellow, a mongoloid,
40 years old, who, being cherished,
learned recently to read and write,
and now has written a poem.
  'Summer in the West when
   everything is quiet
  And clear, with everything
   beautiful and green,
  With wild flowers of all colors,
   and a small water creek,
And a beautiful blue sky. And
  the trees,' he wrote,
forming the letters carefully, his tongue
protruding, 'are very still.
  And sometimes a small breeze.'

He has been cherished,
slowly learned
what many learn fast, and go on

to other knowledge. He
knows nothing of man's devices,
          may die without discovering that
he's dumb, and they
are smart, the killers.

And the uncherished idiots,
tied in cots, smelling
of shit—
          exquisite dumbness,
guaranteed not to know,
ever, how smart
a man can be,
          homo faber of laser beams, of
quaintly-named, flesh-directed, utterly ingenious
mutilating spit-balls,
          yes,
the smartest boys, obedient to all the rules, who never
aimed any flying objects across the classroom,
now are busy with finely calibrated equipment
fashioning spit-balls with needles in them,
that fly at the speed of light multiplied
around corners and into tunnels to arrive
directly at the dumb perfection of living targets,
icily into warm wholeness to fragment it.

We who
          know this
tremble
at our own comprehension.
Are we infected,
viciously, being smart enough
to write down these matters,
          scribes of the unspeakable?
We pray to retain
something round, blunt, soft, slow,
dull in us,
not to sharpen, not to be smart.

In Thai Binh (Peace) Province

for Muriel and Jane

I've used up all my film on bombed hospitals,
bombed village schools, the scattered
lemon-yellow cocoons at the bombed silk-factory,

and for the moment all my tears too
are used up, having seen today
yet another child with its feet blown off,
        a girl, this one, eleven years old,
patient and bewildered in her home, a fragile
small house of mud bricks among rice fields.

So I'll use my dry burning eyes
to photograph within me
dark sails of the river boats,
warm slant of afternoon light
apricot on the brown, swift, wide river,
village towers—church and pagoda—on the far shore,
and a boy and small bird both
perched, relaxed, on a quietly grazing
buffalo.   Peace within the
        long war.

It is that life, unhurried, sure, persistent,
I must bring home when I try to bring
the war home.
        Child, river, light.

Here the future, fabled bird
that has migrated away from America,
nests, and breeds, and sings,

common as any sparrow.

All the while among
the rubble even, and in
the hospitals, among the wounded,
        not only beneath
        lofty clouds

              in temples
            by the shores of lotus-dreaming
            lakes

a fragrance:
flowers, incense, the earth-mist rising
of mild daybreak in the delta—good smell
of life.

It's in America
where no bombs ever
have screamed down smashing
the buildings, shredding the people's bodies,
tossing the fields of Kansas or Vermont or Maryland into
                          the air
to land wrong way up, a gash of earth-guts . . .
it's in America, everywhere, a faint seepage,
I smell death.

Hanoi–Boston–Maine, November 1972

A Poem at Christmas, 1972,
during the Terror-Bombing of North Vietnam

Now I have lain awake imagining murder.
At first my pockets were loaded with rocks, with knives,
wherever I ran windows smashed, but I was swift

and unseen,

    I was saving the knives until I reached
certain men . . .

        Yes, Kissinger's smile faded,
he clutched his belly, he reeled . . .
But as the night
wore on, what I held
hidden—under a napkin perhaps,
    I as a waitress at the inaugural dinner —
was a container of napalm:
and as I threw it in Nixon's face
and his crowd leapt back from the flames with crude

yells of horror,

and some came rushing to seize me:
    quick as thought I had ready
a round of those small bombs designed
to explode at the pressure of a small child's weight,
and these instantly
dealt with the feet of Nixon's friends and henchmen,
who fell in their own blood
while the foul smoke of his body-oils
blackened the hellish room . . .
It was of no interest
to imagine further. Instead,
the scene recommenced.
Each time around, fresh details,
variations of place and weapon.
All night imagining murder.
O, to kill
the killers!

It is
to this extremity

the infection of their evil

thrusts us . . .

Goodbye to Tolerance

Genial poets, pink-faced
earnest wits—
you have given the world
some choice morsels,
gobbets of language presented
as one presents T-bone steak
and Cherries Jubilee.
Goodbye, goodbye,
             I don't care
if I never taste your fine food again,
neutral fellows, seers of every side.
Tolerance, what crimes
are committed in your name.

And you, good women, bakers of nicest bread,
blood donors. Your crumbs
choke me, I would not want
a drop of your blood in me, it is pumped
by weak hearts, perfect pulses that never
falter: irresponsive
to nightmare reality.

It is my brothers, my sisters,
whose blood spurts out and stops
forever
because you choose to believe it is not your business.

Goodbye, goodbye,
your poems
shut their little mouths,
your loaves grow moldy,
a gulf has split
             the ground between us,

and you won't wave, you're looking
another way.
We shan't meet again—
unless you leap it, leaving
behind you the cherished
worms of your dispassion,
your pallid ironies,
your jovial, murderous,
wry-humored balanced judgment,
leap over, un-
balanced? . . . then
how our fanatic tears
would flow and mingle
for joy . . .

January 1973

Dragon of Revolutionary Love

i

All the grievous wounds the murderers
crudely disguised as surgeons, inflict on the innocent—
gouging their flesh and the earth and rivers of their flesh—
are only debridements, light scrapings
of the layer just below the skin.

Breathing their own stale breath inside their masks,
fingers itching in bloody gloves,
they fail to touch the spirit-dragon
alive in the bone and marrow of their prey.

ii

From the Red River's many mouths
uprises
        a spirit-song.
Glittering drops that fall free from the nets
as fishermen take their catch
are the bright scales of the spirit-dragon.

iii

To live
beyond survival.
When a whole child
hurries to school with a legless child
on his back,
both of them flushed with pride,

the spirit-dragon
flies alongside them.

Hanoi, 1972–Temple, Maine, 1973

Wring the swan's neck, seeking
a little language of drops of blood.

How can we speak of blood, the sky
is drenched with it.

A little language
of dew, then.

It dries.

A language
of leaves underfoot.
Leaves on the tree, trembling
in speech. Poplars
              tremble and speak
if you draw near them.

Mycelium, the delicate white threads
mushrooms weave in their chosen earth
(or manure or leafmold) to grow from

and milkweed silk orioles knit
into hammock nests their eggs
lilt in

and silver timbers
of old barns near salt water—

all of these
dreamed of, woven, knit, mitered
into a vision named 'A Visit Home'
(as if there were a home I had,
beyond the houses I live in, or those
I've lived in and hold
dimly in mind)
                    that waking
shook apart, out of
coherence, unwove, unraveled, took
beam by beam away, splintered.

More real than ever, as I move
in the world, and never out of it,
Solitude.

Typewriter, telephone, ugly names
of things we use, I use. Among them, though,
float milkweed silks.

Like a mollusk's, my hermitage
is built of my own cells.
Burned faces, stretched horribly,

eyes and mouths forever open,
weight the papers down on my desk.
No day for years I have not thought of them.

And more true than ever the familiar image
placing love on a border
where, solitary, it paces, exchanging
across the line a deep attentive gaze
with another solitude pacing there.

Yet almost no day, too, with no
happiness, no
exaltation of larks uprising from the heart's
peat-bog darkness.

At the door, some *never,* some *let it be,*
those pestering halftruths of impatience . . .

Yet the daily bread gets baked,
a rush of initiative takes the stairs
three at a time.
                  Crippled by their feet,
the swans waddle to water,
the first of them already
slowly and silently has ripped the silk of evening.

When I am the sky
a glittering bird
slashes at me with the knives of song.

When I am the sea
fiery clouds plunge into my mirrors,
fracture my smooth breath with crimson sobbing.

When I am the earth
I feel my flesh of rock wearing down:
pebbles, grit, finest dust, nothing.

When I am a woman—O, when I am
a woman,
my wells of salt brim and brim,
poems force the lock of my throat.

It is the one in homespun
you hunger for
when you are lonesome;

the one in crazy feathers
dragging opal chains in dust
wearies you

wearies herself perhaps
but has to drive on
clattering rattletrap into

fiery skies for trophies,
into the blue that is bluer
because of the lamps,

the silence keener because it is solitude
moving through multitude on the night streets.

But the one in homespun
whom you want is weary
too, wants to sit down

beside you neither silent
nor singing, in quietness. Alas,
they are not two but one,

pierce the flesh of one, the other
halfway across the world, will shriek,
her blood will run. Can you endure
life with two brides, bridegroom?

i

With dread she heard the letter
fall into the drop.

       Playing frisbee
    turns out to be a graceful merriment,
    almost like chasing butterflies.
Even she herself
could not have said for sure, as she played,
the letter was moving north already
to indict her history.

Decision, and fear, and then—
a picnic.
    'If I should come upon myself
suddenly,' she thinks, 'nothing would show I knew the
                        letter was crawling
grayly north to pronounce sentence,
to send a lifetime out into exile.'

    Magically the tangerine disc
    glides and curves and chooses
    to land in someone's outflung hand, sometimes
    even in unpracticed hers; gracious caprice.
Or circles back to fingers that sent it forth.
The game is a dance.
            Incandescent
the round charcoals, lambent
the white ash.
        Sun's fire
scatters between dark branches for those few
    passionate moments it takes each night to say
    farewell, and drop
            over the world's edge.

Laughter around the picnic table
lightly skims the ungathered dusk.

ii

Two letters passed each other, carried
north and south.
In the first was written: 'Our journey has come to a dead end,
we mustn't cower by that wall,
skin our fingers trying to scale it,
batter shoulder and head pushing against it,
perish there.
I have come to believe
it towers to the sky
and is thick through with layers of stone to the horizon.
We can only admit defeat,
and the road being closed to us by which we came—
closed like an ocean-furrow—
now we must each take one of the narrow paths,
left and right, parallel
to the wall at first,
then bearing away from it,
                              wider and wider apart
from it and from
each other.'
                    In the second letter was written
'We must return
to sunrise and morning freshness, to seeing
one
another
anew.
        When I'm clear,
I see you, when I see you
I love you. How much life
we have lived together. Life begins
to wake new in me.'

55

The first letter is still
on its way, the second
has been received.
> They are two songs
> each in a different key,
> two fables told
> in different countries,
> two pairs of eyes looking past each other
> to different distances.

Summer 1972

Lily Bloom, what ominous fallen crowfeathers of shadow
the nightlight scattered around your outspread hair
on feverish cumulus of pillows—
demonic darkness, hair, feathers, jabs of greenish
sickroom light.
                    And your sallow face, long, lost, lonely,
O Lily Bloom, dying,
                    looked into mine those nights,
searching, equine, for life to be lived—
but not believing. Believing yourself fit for the knacker's yard . . .

What I told you—promised you—
though I meant it, didn't make sense:
Friendship, Life of Art, Love of Nature.
You had no correlatives, I had
no holiness.
You saved me the exact shame of not coming across. But Lily—
whom I remember not in my head (or barely once a year)
but in my nerves—what brimming measure of living
your death exacts from me! And when the fire of me smokes
or gasps as flames will do when a contending element
chokes their utterance, and they burn livid instead of red,

then I know I am cheating you. Living this half-life in my
                                        fiftieth year
cheats you. If I can't give you water, give myself
water, then I must give you, give myself, some icy spirits,
diamonds on the tongue,
                    to sear cracked lips and
                    quicken the heart: a ceremony
of living.
Love, lovers, husband, child, land and ocean, struggle and solitude:
you've had these, and more, but you need more.

                              We have other years
to go, Lily. I thirst too.
                         We're not free
of our covenant, Enemy, Burden, Friend.

Living Alone (I)

In this silvery now of living alone,
doesn't it seem, I ponder,
anything can happen?
On the flat roof of a factory
at eye level from my window,
starling naiads dip in tremulous rainpools
where the sky floats, and is no smaller
than long ago.
Any strange staircase, as if I were twenty-one—
any hand drawing me up it,
could lead me to my life.
Some days.

And if I coast, down toward home, spring evenings, silently,
a kind of song rising in me to encompass
Davis Square and the all-night
cafeteria and the pool hall,
it is childhood's song, surely no note is changed,
sung in Valentines Park or on steep streets in the map of my mind
in the hush of suppertime, everyone gone indoors.
Solitude within multitude seduced me early.

Some days, though,
living alone,
there's only knowledge of silence,
clutter of bells cobwebbed
in crumbling belfry,
words jaggéd,
in midutterance broken.

Starlings, as before,
whistle wondering at themselves,
crescendo, diminuendo.
My heart pounds away,
confident as a clock.
Yet there is silence.

New leafed, the neighbor trees
round out. There's one,
near my window,
seems to have no buds, though.

I said, the summer garden I planted
bears only leaves—leaves in abundance—
but no flowers.
And then the flowers,
        many colors and forms,
        subtle, mysterious,
came forth.

I said, the tree has no buds.
And then the leaves,
        shyly, sparse, as if reluctant,
in less than two days appeared,
and the tree, now,
        is flying on green wings.

What magic denial
shall my life utter
to bring itself forth?

for Mitch

i.   The Cloud

We have entered sadness
as one enters a mountain cloud.

One stands in the midst of rain that is not raining.
Summits vanish, sheepdog's bark is dim.

Move and the cloud moves too,
and sighs with a million infinitesimal white breaths.

In single file, slowly,
clouds take to the sheep paths,

cloudy sadness, vague arms around us,
carries us like a bundle.

ii.   The Recollection

There was once a cloud—remember?
—with swift undulations drew away from our feet,
revealed that where we stood edged a precipice:

and deep below was a radiant valley,
rivers, fold and fields, gleaming villages.

iii.   The Cutting-beam

Imagine this blur of chill, white, gray, vague, sadness
burned off.

Imagine a landscape
of dry clear sunlight, precise shadows,
forms of pure color.

Imagine two neighboring hills, and
your house, my house, looking across, friendly:
imagine ourselves
meeting each other,
bringing gifts, bringing news.

Yes, we need the heat
of imagination's sun
to cut through our bonds of cloud.

And oh, can the great and golden light
warm our flesh that has grown so cold?

The 4 a.m. freight comes pounding and shaking through
                                        the fall night
and I go to the Middle Door to watch,
                        through the plain glass that has
                                stained glass around it,
pressing my forehead against the pane,

and Steve hurries along to look too—for he's out of Appalachia,
the lonesome romance of the rails West is in his bones;

and Richard comes close behind, gazing intently
                                over my shoulder—
out of the Midwest and the rails West are in his blood,
and our friend Bo is at this very moment hopping freight in Oregon
                                to pick pears;

and I seem to smell iron and rust, an animal smell,
                                red and dusty,
even through the glass that's steaming up with our breaths.
So I start to open the door, to hear the last cars and the
                                caboose louder
and the sound of going away, and to see the stars,

and I want you, Mitch, to step out with me into the dark garden,
for you're standing back of me too, taller than anyone;

but as the cold air comes in I turn toward you and you're
                                not there.
Then I realize I'm waking up: the train really is going by
but the Middle Door's back in my childhood, not in America,

and there's no one in the house but you and me,
you asleep beside me in bed, and soon you'll have left

and this moment of dark boxcars just visible
under the paling stars, a train of looming forms from
                                        faraway states
lurching through the edge of Boston,

is just the beginning of a long train of times I'll turn
to share a vision with you and find I'm dreaming.

September 6–7, 1974

One garland
of flowers, leaves, thorns
was twined round our two necks.
Drawn tight, it could choke us,
yet we loved its scratchy grace,
our fragrant yoke.

We were Siamese twins.
Our blood's not sure
if it can circulate,
now we are cut apart.
Something in each of us is waiting
to see if we can survive,
severed.

A virtuoso dog at midnight—high wavering howl
resolved in three staccato low barks.
Three times the same utterance
repeated, insisted on.
It makes sure, like a bird practicing,
           through the day,
           its phrase.
I listen half asleep, aware
of pleasure in listening,
not afraid of my solitude.
Yet the fear nags me: is the wound
my life has suffered
           healing too fast,
shutting in bad blood?
Will the scar
pucker the skin of my soul?
'Shut up,' someone shouts at the dog
who again lifts his complaint
into the fall night in strange song.

When your voice breaks
I'm impaled on the jaggéd
edges of its fracture.

It is visible
to mind's eye, bone or grained
splintering wood.

Bone-voice, O wooden
sobbing. The flesh of my spirit
is sore. I'm powerless

to mend you. Marrow,
or sap rising in the fibers
that hold, must do it.

I suffer
less your pain than my
helplessness,

hoisted off the
earth of my energies like
a bug overturned,

feet waving
wild and feeble.

Raising our glasses, smilingly
we wish one another not luck
but happiness. After half a lifetime
with and without luck,
we know we need more than luck.
It makes no difference that we're drinking
tomato juice, not wine or whiskey—
we know what we mean,
and the red juice of those virtuous
vegetable-fruits is something we both enjoy.
I remember your wonder, as at a miracle,
finding them growing on sturdy vines
in my old aunt and uncle's sun-room
ripe to pluck at the breakfast table!
We were twenty-three, and unappeasably hungry . . .

We agree on tomatoes, then—and happiness?
yes, that too: we mean growth, branching,
leafing, yielding blossoms and fruit and the sharp odor
                                 of dreams.
We mean knowing someone as deeply,
no, deeper, than we've known each other,
we mean being known. We are wishing each other
the luck not to need luck. I mill
some pepper into my juice, though,
and salt in the ancient gesture; and what would be wrong
with tipping out half a glass
for the gods?
                We smile.
After these months of pain we begin
to admit our new lives have begun.

February 1975

SEVEN

Seth Thomas: A Love Poem

for Fran and Tom

Rejoining Time after fifty years,
not slow, not fast.
Pendulum beaming gold in miniature cupboard.
Confident lame tock *tock*.
Melodious chime of three at one a.m.,
midnight at seven.

i

Trees that lift themselves like clouds
above the woods,

crest of the woods and then
more, a breath

in winter air, a web.
of fiber, from afar

so tenuous, near
a stiff hard complication

of live sticks.

ii

Eve's lavender
from a garden gone
                    seven years now
under concrete—

fragrant.
                (The church wanted
                money: but Eve,
                moneyless, with a poet's
                humor, or lack of it,

                did not waste the pink
                Thank Offering envelope,

'To Be Used Any Time God Has Blessed You,'

ideal for mailing lavender,
mint leaves, or winged seeds

when the spirit
                    moved her.)

iii

Encircling gold faded
to gray, stalks
tough still but leaves
frost bitten,

what large brown faces
—smiling,
seedy—
the sunflowers have.

iv

Which of them has it
it's too soon to tell—

David, John,
      Naomi, Carlene . . .

Confusion, growth, the analogies
perceived.   Seed of words
that didn't come up three
or five or seven
years back putting out

green shoots now, small
sturdy shrubs, vine tangles not resembling
remembered cotyledons.
                            Paul, Andrea, Aaron . . .
Letters
come in from
                    far away
as if in bottles.
                    (What was
the ancient children's game,
some token
concealed and passed
from hand to hand? Pincushion, button, ring—
some common
talisman . . .)

Flames upspring
feline
        to illumine
one face or another, moments
of profound chiaroscuro,
definition of feature—

but not yet
from inside out through their skulls
or through one skull
persistently

the fiery moonlight,
            the tattered rage
                of the sun . . .

i

He picks up crystal buttons from the ocean floor.
Gills of the mind pulse in unfathomed water.

In the infinite dictionary he discovers
gold grains of sand. Each has its twin
on some shore the other side of the world.

Blind to what he does not yet need,
he feels his way over broken glass
to the one stone that fits his palm.

When he opens his eyes he gives to what he gazes at
the recognition no look ever before granted it.
It becomes a word. Shuddering, it takes wing.

ii

> 'What is to give light must endure burning.'
> Viktor Frankl, *The Doctor and the Soul*

Blind until dreaming gray
sparks green, his eyes
set fire to an ashen street,
a dancer's
bitter flesh in daybreak,
the moon's
last noontime look
over its shoulder.
They fade; the flames
go on burning,
enduring.

iii

Deaf till he hears
what answers:
     Grandfatherly
bell, tolling
and telling
of faithful Time, that flood
(ever-rolling), of faithful blood.
The answers pushing
boundaries over,
(those proud embankments),
the asking revealed.

The asking, stones
bared of earth,
hammers at the door, a pulse
in the temple:
the insistent dance
of Who and How and Where,
the arms-akimbo of When.

iv

One at a time
books, when their hour is come
step out of the shelves.
Heavily step (once more, dusty, fingermarked,
     but pristine!)
to give birth:

each poem's passion
ends in an Easter,
a new life.

The books of the dead
shake their leaves,
word-seeds fly and
lodge in the black earth.

v

Coffee cups fall out of his hands,
doorknobs slip his grasp and
doors slam,
antique writing desks break under his
leaning elbows—Taurus
is bucking and thudding, head down across
the cramped field.
                    But scraps of wood
found on the street, one night when winds were
scraping the thick dark to a steely shine,
                    become in the poet's hands
a table,
        round and
set firm on its one leg.

vi

To make poems is to find
an old chair in the gutter
and bring it home
into the upstairs cave;
a stray horse from the pound,
a stray boat on the weedy shore,
phosphorescent.

Then in the broken rocking chair
take off—to reality!
Realm of ambrosia and hard crusts
earnest trudging doesn't lead to.

Only when feet begin
to dance, when the chair
creaks and gallops,
do the gates open
and we
            discover ourselves
inside
the kingless kingdom.

vii

The wild moonbull
                        who is the poet
grazes alone
a field of infinite, dewdrenched,
drops of red clover,
sharp spears of grass
                        which are words.

Over the barbed fence a troop
of boys and young men
                        who are the poet
throng,
            breathless, silent,
to the encounter.

They desire
to practice the dance.
Secretly to prepare.

He breathes
his green, fresh, breath at them,
still distant,
gazing innocent
through full-moon silver
toward them
and viciously
rushes them, they step
each aside,
old coats for capes,
they taunt him,
he tosses
his deadly flourish of horns,
they love him, they imagine
the hot sunlight of the sacred kill.

Implacable silver
fades. By moonset

they vanish, he hears
the wire fence
twang where they climbed it.

viii

Shadowdog
blocking the threshold.
Only a shadow. But
bites!
     Try
to get out, try
to get in:

      the obstacle
sinks its
teeth in
flesh, and

blood flows,
they are not
shadowteeth,
are sharp, and
dirty.

      •

The venom rises
from torn foot to
heart. Makes
a knot in the heart.

A screeching:
of brakes on the street,
of an unsuspected
voice outcrying
through the poet's
lips, denying
poetry,
        violent
palpitating beat of
the mind's wings caged.

Dust on the tongue.

Storm
of torn feathers.

Falling.
      Falling—

Hassidic rocking
is always back and forth,
       back and forth,
in perfect measure with the words,
over and over,
every day of the year—

except one:

on the day the Temple is destroyed
     which is also
the day the Messiah is born,
on that day alone, the rocking
moves from side to side,
        side to side,
a swaying,
as trees sway in the wind.

x

On his one leg that aches
the poet
learns to stand firm
upholding
the round table of his
blank page.
When the wind blows
his wood
shall be tree again.
Shall stir,
shall sigh and sing.

'Whatever has black sounds, has *duende.*'
Manuel Torres, quoted by Federico García Lorca

And now the sounds
are green, a snowdrop's quiet
defiant insignia:

and now the sounds
crackle with mica glitterings,
rasp with cinder,
call with the oboe calm of rose quartz:

and now the sounds
are bone flutes, echo
from deepest canyon, sounds
only the earliest, palest stars may hear:

and now the sounds
are black. Are black sounds.
Black. The deep song
delves.

Red wine
            from the
                        Black Sea.
                                    Glasses
filled and refilled,
Georgian shishkebab has been eaten,
                                    plates pushed back, voices
of other diners surround us—

Sometimes the five of us speak at once, so much is lost,
                                                we are all
in our forties, it is perhaps ten at night—

the woman who is
                        our interpreter
                        knows, she knows
poignantly: now is the night she must speak for us—

People look round to see who's come in, all
members of the tribe of the word. Chairs are pushed back,
                                                swing door
lets out moments of kitchen clatter—
                        She knows she must *be*
each of us turn by turn and
each at once.

I see their eyes:

The fat poet I barely know, but surely
love,
who pours the wine
quietly, his eyes
kind, small, and sorrowful.

Blue, blue eyes in a tanned face, the veriest *azure* eyes
I've looked to ever: the poet's trusted friend; historian,
fresh from the re-examined lives of the Nihilists.

(Will you have ice cream?—the waiters
returning and leaving again)—

                  Pale eyes of the biologist, pale face,
white beard,
though not old. He's O.K.,
a good guy—
but the others
know things he doesn't know.
He has
an aura of limits . . .

And I, I'm looking
from one to the other, trying to read
language in gesture, grasping
what Russian words I know, turning
to her who so often
looks either acutely anxious or deeply amused—
my sister the medium—interpretress! Oracle!—to give me
what these brothers are saying (for there's a spirit
has touched us, pulled us
suddenly close).

              Frown-lines and laugh-lines leave her face,
she is looking
            upward through smoke to the high ceiling,
                and through it
                    searching—

'Each cell,' the biologist says, 'has in it
the whole body's potential.'

                    (And I think of the module, of detail
              giving to inscape its signature, the great
                    web of analogy)—
but it seems he implies
some kind of determinism (I've been saying
I don't see *enough* communism here, no struggling toward
a classless society). Communism to him
is only the best we can do
with the historic, the social, shell, in which
the creature lives
                    unregenerate.
                              The historian faults him,
but I lose that, people come by, greetings exchanged—

Red wine from the black sea.
She searches
and finds the eloquent, accurate words of translation:
                                        the poet now
out of his stillness is talking: 'Poems,' he says,
'poems are of two kinds: those with mystery,
                    those without mystery.'
'And are poems without mystery poems at all?' 'Well . . . yes;
one cannot say
a poem wellmade, effective, but unmysterious,
has no value. But for myself—
I prefer the mysterious . . .'
                    'And Dostoyevsky—
why is it he, who's so often
clearly reactionary, pessimistic, all for
personal redemption and against
common action—antirevolutionary!—why is it he's
the 19th-century writer I see is most read, most loved,
in the Soviet Union?—Whereas Turgeniev, for instance,
whose work surely—(I think of the *Sportsman's Sketches*
                              especially)—'

'*Ah!* But Dostoyevsky!' (Historian and poet, both are speaking)
'Who reached as he did into the hot and strange—'
                                        'the cold and shadowy—'
'the intricate depths of life? We read him—'
                                        'We read him because:
in him—'
            '—in him we know
our own darknesses and illuminations,
tortures and ecstasies: our human reality.'

Tea in glasses. Thick black coffee. Vodka? Vodka.
'To *Serve the People*,' I venture, 'is often thought of
—wrongly, narrowly—merely as mutual encouragement.
But to serve the people in truth one must do, I think,
what Pasternak said one must do: *excel oneself
in order to be oneself.*'
                                        'To serve the people,' (the poet again
holds us in his hands, we are listening shells to whom
a heartbeat speaks),
                                        'to serve the people
one must write for the ideal reader. Only for the ideal reader.
And who or what is that ideal reader? God. One must imagine,
one must deeply *imagine*
                                        that great Attention.
Only so,
in lonely dialogue, can one reach—
the people.'

After our musing silences
have traveled away, each on its own road,
and returned again to this night, this place
of meeting—island of our eternity in the bustle and clatter
of passing time—now the biologist
(pale, skeptical, yet a friend: I see he's at bottom innocent
as only the trained skeptic can be,
whose imagination
is weak as fine hair) is telling,

88

when I've asked if anyone reads Kropotkin, that,
'Lenin said, after he'd talked for hours with Kropotkin,
What a charming old man! and shook his head, and added,
But he understands nothing. Nothing. But later Lenin sent
a train, a special train back and forth to the place where he,
the old man, lay dying, only to ask each day after him . . .'

He smiles, he is pale and gentle.
                              'To me it seems,'
I say, going slowly, waiting for her: she's ready:
'To me it seems perhaps
Kropotkin understood half
                              of what we need to know,
and Lenin perhaps
knew half, and true revolution . . . true revolution
must put these two halves together?'

                              A flash
                              of sapphire!
                  I hear
                  the historian's words, and understand them,
                  and wonder:
my woman friend
repeats in English, 'How young! How pure!'

I'm abashed, though he is speaking
without mockery, almost tenderly.
                              'I young, pure? Why, I'm two years older
than our friend here, the poet . . . And what have I spoken of
but doubts, of perplexity?'
'Human doubts, human longing,' he utters the words
solemnly,—'human longing
                              for ineffable justice and mercy:
in these lies purity
and the worth of men's lives—
new as a birch bud in spring.'

His mind has touched, moved into and out of,
as if into seacarved hollows bristling with hidden spines,
                                            venomous tentacles,
                        the life of Nechaev,
                        killer, shaman. He has known
                        the sacrament of the absolute.

    And then he says,
                        'In the end
we must follow Christ.' 'Is he joking?'—
                        I turn to my woman friend again, confused.
'No. No,' the historian says, understanding my question,
'I am not joking. I'm speaking
of spirit. Not dogma but spirit. The Way.'

                            (Not the corrupt Church—
            bejeweled priests with dirty beards
            prostrating themselves before the atrocious Czars—
    its indispensable beggars encrusting the entrances
    of every shrine, kissing with pus
    the infinite insensibility of relics.

                        Not this but
                        the frail trust we have
                    when our hearts flutter, and we look
                    each to each,
                    and our eyes hold.
                                        The Way.)
And the poet—it's midnight, the room is half empty, soon
                                        we must part—
the poet, his presence
ursine and kind, shifting his weight in a chair too small
                                        for him,
quietly says, and shyly: 'The Poet
                    never must lose despair.'

Then our eyes indeed
meet and hold.
                    All of us know, smiling
in common knowledge—
even the palest spirit among us, burdened
as he is with weight of abstractions—
                    all of us know he means
we mustn't, any of us, lose touch with the source,
pretend it's not there, cover over
the mineshaft of passion
                              despair somberly tolls its bell
                                        from the depths of,
and wildest joy
sings out of too,
               flashing
                         the scales of its laughing, improbable
                                                      music,

grief and delight entwined in the dark down there.

'The Poem Rising By Its Own Weight'

The poet is at the disposal of his own night.
Jean Cocteau

The singing robes fly onto your body and cling there silkily,
you step out on the rope and move unfalteringly across it,

and seize the fiery knives unscathed and
keep them spinning above you, a fountain
of rhythmic rising, falling, rising
flames,

and proudly let the chains
be wound about you, ready
to shed them, link by steel link,
padlock by padlock—

                    but when your graceful
confident shrug and twist drives the metal
into your flesh and the python grip of it tightens
and you see rust on the chains and blood in your pores
and you roll
over and down a steepness into a dark hole
and there is not even the sound of mockery in the distant air
somewhere above you where the sky was,
no sound but your own breath panting:
then it is that the miracle
walks in, on his swift feet,
down the precipice straight into the cave,
opens the locks,
knots of chain fall open,
twists of chain unwind themselves,
links fall asunder,
in seconds there is a heap of scrap-
metal at your ankles, you step free and at once
he turns to go—

but as you catch at him with a cry,
clasping his knees, sobbing your gratitude,
with what radiant joy he turns to you,
and raises you to your feet,
and strokes your disheveled hair,
and holds you,
        holds you,
            holds you
close and tenderly before he vanishes.

EIGHT

Prayer for Revolutionary Love

That a woman not ask a man to leave meaningful work to
                                        follow her.
That a man not ask a woman to leave meaningful work to
                                        follow him.

That no one try to put Eros in bondage.
But that no one put a cudgel in the hands of Eros.

That our loyalty to one another and our loyalty to our work
not be set in false conflict.

That our love for each other give us love for each other's work.
That our love for each other's work give us love for one another.

That our love for each other's work give us love for one another.
That our love for each other give us love for each other's work.

That our love for each other, if need be,
give way to absence. And the unknown.

That we endure absence, if need be,
without losing our love for each other.
Without closing our doors to the unknown.

Modes of Being

for Nguyen Cong Hoan

January's fist
unclenches.
        Walls of brick
are bastions of coral, welltempered, basking,
and shadows yawn and
stretch to the east.
           Watching the afternoon,
from the window watching it slowly brim
and not spill, not yet, into evening,
soothes and gives pleasure.

                Near Saigon,
                in a tiger-cage, a man
                tries to stretch out his hand
                and cannot.

Indoors, reading, talking,
we reach and enter
           a new landscape of knowledge,
as if coming through a high mountain pass together,
that wonder of other flora, different
ways of constructing rooves and
terracing fields, the haymakers
dressed differently.
           What more
can love be than epiphany!

                Near Saigon,
                in a tiger-cage, a woman
                tries to straighten her
                      cramped spine
                and cannot.

Unclenched fist,
cinnamon warmth of winter light,
revelation, communion . . .
Unable
      to know for long
what we know; neither intense love
nor intense pain. Nature itself
allows the delight of sparrows
ruffling an inchdeep lake of rain
in the jailhouse yard.
                Joy
is real, torture
is real, we strain to hold
a bridge between them open,
and fail,
or all but fail.

        Near Saigon, in cages
        made in America, jailers
        force fluid down the prisoners' throats,
        stomp on their swollen bellies.
        This has been happening
        for a long time.
        This is happening
        now, while I write, January
        nineteen seventy-four.

What wings, what mighty arch
of feathered hollow bones, beyond
span of albatross or eagle,
mind and heart must grow
                to touch, trembling,
with outermost pinion tips,
not in alternation but both at once,
in one
violent eternal instant
that which is and
that which is . . .

A Letter to Marek about a Photograph

for Mark Pawlak

This carpentered, unpainted, aging house,
one of many alike in some white ghetto,
is filled to the uninsulated seams with a face:
the brooding face of anxiety.   —Or the house
(one cannot say which is
superimposed on the other) is so montaged,
waking and sleeping, into that mind, it is
the house fills the outgazing head,
extends its boundaries with wooden angles.
                                        And the face
is the face of your father, Marek,
a Polish workman, or of his brother, or—
for, beardless and hair dragged back,
it could be the face of a woman—your mother,
your grandmother in the 1930's,
just staying off the breadline . . .
any young woman quickly grown old, forehead
deeply wrinkled, eyes unable to laugh. Whatever else
—store-boughten furnishings, tawdry treasures, stories—
is inside the house, at the door
that *look* looks out,
worry without hope.
                          But the house itself
though cheaply built, has its share of ornaments turned on the lathe
of humor and trust, a human, unique
identity fronting the weather. In houses like these
your family of millions, Polacks, Wops,
Scotch-Irish, people shut now into 'projects,'
used to live. You would have known its
familiar mystery, its faint, sour charm,
even by dark, even before you had seen
its fretted gable, Marek:

your in-feeling comprehension
would touch with probing finger
the concealed wounds of those who built,
those who dwelt, those who moved on
or died here. Your gift is to reveal
poetry in the cries caught in nameless throats,
in eyes gazing into the street of trouble,
and foolish tender joys suspended
in half-light of memory; to lift
griefs out of the blind pit of unknowing,
placing glass and mercury under the tongue of dreams—
magical quick-
silver that measures
the fever it is to be human.

Room

for D. Mitchell and D. Hass

Shelf of worn, chipped, exquisite china oddments,
for daily use.
Baskets, for fruit, potatoes, shopping.
Stove with grill where David
makes such good brown toast.
Left of the sink, above the counter,
Mary Wolstonecraft, fair face, dark shadows, energy.
Slightly unsteady, the small table. Notes to each other,
and soon, when David and David come home,
strong cups of tea.
It's the kitchen, its window viewless,
and not the handsome calm of the living room,
I find myself in, at peace,
though the presence across the hall of
that room too is part of being here:
the threadbare gracious carpet,
surreal romances of the Victorian *découpage* screen,
poplars and oaks and sunsets the large windows look to.
Afternoon, an ample easy quiet.

                          But it breaks

sharply: the Davids
have moved, all the objects
stand at new angles, a kitchen I've never seen,
light from another compass point.
This room, my refuge, is nowhere but in my mind,
more blurred for them than for me, their memories
too many to sift and focus. 'Bees of the invisible,'
take this nectar, transform it, internalize it! If I lose
the knowledge of this place,
my soul shall be diminished. There is a song in all
humankind, that rooms, houses, parks, streets, fields
and particular corners of fields, rivers and certain

102

eye-span reaches of rivers, are notes in, as people are.
Give me the power
to sound this note, the disappeared-
as-if-torn-down, but clear, cool, tranquil kitchen
on Downside Crescent present in me,
a place to *be* in, not pretending
no tears were shed in it, no hard words ever shouted,
no gray mornings caught in the small mirror over the sink—
but seeing despite that, precisely because of that,
(grief not being turned away, a place
made for grief to be) one could
be there, and breathe easy, uncrowded.
A note or chord of notes
sustained, hushing, recurrent
in the stream of song.

for Barbara Fussiner and Richard Edelman

Fluttering strips of paper strung on cord
tied to the ship's rail.
Each inscribed.
Read them:

'How deep the waves' blue!'

'How bright the foam!'

'Wind and light
sparkle together!'

'How the sea's plumage
preens itself!'

These are prayers.
To celebrate,
not to beseech.
Among them, leaning
toward the water, we voyage,
are voyaged, seeing.
We share among us
the depth of day, are borne
through it
swiftly as arcs of spray.

Salt glitters
on our lips,
on ruffled paper. Soon
the words will fly on their torn strips
beyond vision.

Silent, smiling, receiving
joyfully what we are given,
we utter
each to each
our absolute presence.

Tasted (and spat out)
Satan's Boletus.
Delicious!

I asked a blind man the way east,
because I'd not seen him,
not looked before asking.
He smiled, and walked on,
sure of his felt way,
silent.

Their high pitched baying
as if in prayer's unison

remote, undistracted, given over
utterly to belief,

the skein of geese
voyages south,
           hierarchic arrow of its convergence toward
           the point of grace
swinging and rippling, ribbon tail
of a kite, loftily

over lakes where they have not
elected to rest,

over men who suppose
earth is man's, over golden earth

preparing itself
for night and winter.
             We humans
are smaller than they, and crawl
unnoticed,

about and about the smoky map.

Perhaps we humans
have wanted God most as witness
to acts of choice
made in solitude. Acts of mercy,
of sacrifice. Wanted
that great single eye to see us,
steadfast as we flowed by.
Yet there are other acts
not even vanity,
or anxious hope to please, knows of—
bone doings, leaps of nerve, heart-
cries of communion: if there is bliss,
it has
been already
and will be; out-
reaching, utterly.
Blind
to itself, flooded
with otherness.

Fixed unchanged — *Emptiness*

Unwrap the dust from its mummycloths.
Let Ariel learn
a blessing for Caliban
and Caliban drink dew from the lotus
open upon the waters.
Bitter the slow
river water: dew
shall wet his lips with light.
Let the dust
float, the wrappings too
are dust.
      Drift upon the stir
of air, of dark
river: ashes of what had lived,
        or seeds
      of ancient sesame,
      or namelessly
pure dust that is all
in all.   Bless,
weightless Spirit. Drink,
Caliban, push your tongue
heavy into the calyx.

How gray and hard the brown feet of *the wretched of the earth*.
How confidently the crippled from birth
push themselves through the streets, deep in their lives.
How seamed with lines of fate the hands
of women who sit at streetcorners
offering seeds and flowers.
How lively their conversation together.
How much of death they know.
I am tired of 'the fine art of unhappiness.'

New Directions Paperbooks

Complete descriptive catalog available free on request from
New Directions, 333 Sixth Avenue, New York 10014.   † Bilingual